Mighty Machines

Humvees

by Matt Doeden

Consulting Editor: Gail Saunders-Smith, PhD

Consultant: John Grady
Director of Communications
Association of the United States Army

Capstone
press

Mankato, Minnesota

Pebble Plus is published by Capstone Press,
151 Good Counsel Drive, P.O. Box 669, Mankato, Minnesota 56002.
www.capstonepress.com

1 2 3 4 5 6 12 11 10 09 08 07

Library of Congress Cataloging-in-Publication Data
Doeden, Matt
    Humvees / by Matt Doeden
    p. cm.—(Pebble plus. Mighty machines)
    Summary: "Simple text and photographs describe Humvees, their parts, and what they do"—Provided
by publisher.
    Includes bibliographical references and index.
    ISBN-13: 978-1-4296-0030-9 (hardcover)
    ISBN-10: 1-4296-0030-6 (hardcover)
    1. Hummer trucks—Juvenile literature. 2. Military trucks—United States—Juvenile literature. I. Title.
II. Series.
UG618.D64 2008
623.7'4772—dc22   2006101330

Editorial Credits
Mari Schuh and Christopher L. Harbo, editors; Patrick D. Dentinger, book designer; Jo Miller, photo researcher

Photo Credits
AM General Corporation, LLC/Rob Wurtz, cover, 1, 4–5, 7, 8–9, 10–11, 18–19, 20–21
DVIC/LCPL Bobby J. Segovia, USMC, 14–15; LCPL Marcus D. Henry, USMC, 12–13
Photo by Ted Carlson/Fotodynamics, 17

HUMVEE is a registered trademark of AM General LLC.

Note to Parents and Teachers

The Mighty Machines set supports national social studies standards related to science,
technology, and society. This book describes and illustrates Humvees. The images
support early readers in understanding the text. The repetition of words and phrases
helps early readers learn new words. This book also introduces early readers to subject-
specific vocabulary words, which are defined in the Glossary section. Early readers may
need assistance to read some words and to use the Table of Contents, Glossary, Read
More, Internet Sites, and Index sections of the book.

Table of Contents

What Are Humvees?

Humvees are
useful Army vehicles.
The Army uses Humvees
for different missions.

Humvee Parts

Many Humvees

are covered in armor.

Metal plates protect

the crew inside.

7

Humvees sit on big tires.

They travel over

almost any surface.

Big engines make

Humvees move fast.

Humvees have mounts
to hold machine guns
and grenade launchers.

mount

13

What Humvees Do

Humvees carry

troops or cargo.

Humvees work as ambulances.

They rush hurt soldiers

to hospitals.

Humvees go on missions.

They help soldiers watch

and learn about enemies.

Mighty Machines

Humvees speed over
rough ground.
Humvees are
mighty machines.

Glossary

ambulance—a vehicle that takes sick, hurt, or wounded people to a hospital

armor—a Humvee's metal covering; armor protects the crew from bullets and small explosions.

army—a group of soldiers trained to fight on land

cargo—items or goods carried by a vehicle

crew—a team of people who work together

grenade—a small bomb that can be thrown or launched

Humvee—a kind of truck the Army and the Marine Corps use for many kinds of missions; Humvee is a short name for High Mobility Multipurpose Wheeled Vehicle.

machine gun—a gun that can quickly fire many bullets

mission—a special job or task

mount—a metal support to which weapons are attached

troop—a group of soldiers

Read More

Budd, E. S. *Humvees.* Military Machines at Work. Chanhassen, Minn.: Child's World, 2002.

Doeden, Matt. *The U.S. Army.* The U.S. Armed Forces. Mankato, Minn.: Capstone Press, 2005.

Piehl, Janet. *Humvees.* Pull Ahead Books. Minneapolis: Lerner, 2006.

Internet Sites

FactHound offers a safe, fun way to find Internet sites related to this book. All of the sites on FactHound have been researched by our staff.

Here's how:

1. Visit *www.facthound.com*

2. Choose your grade level.

3. Type in this book ID **1429600306** for age-appropriate sites. You may also browse subjects by clicking on letters, or by clicking on pictures and words.

4. Click on the **Fetch It** button.

FactHound will fetch the best sites for you!

Index

Word Count: 87
Grade: 1
Early-Intervention Level: 18